This book belongs to
_____

Harriet Tubman

By Mary Nhin

This book is dedicated to my children - Mikey, Kobe, and Jojo.

Copyright © 2023 by Grow Grit Press LLC. All rights reserved. No part of this book may be reproduced in any form without permission in writing from the publisher. Please send bulk order requests to growgritpress@gmail.com Printed and bound in the USA. MiniMovers.tv
Paperback ISBN: 978-1-63731-675-7   Hardcover ISBN: 978-1-63731-677-1

Hi, I'm Harriet Tubman.

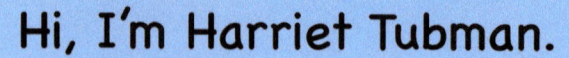

I was born into slavery with my eight siblings.

One day, when I was sent to do an errand, I got hit with a large metal object.

This caused me to have sleeping spells which limited the kind of jobs I could do. Everything changed when I was able to work as a wood cutter with my father, Ben Ross.

As a wood cutter, I learned about secret communication networks from the slaves that gathered the wood.

This helped me dream of freedom and equality.

In 1844, I worked alongside a free black man named John Tubman. We got married and I changed my name to Harriet in honor of my mother.

In 1849, my slave owner died and I was frightened that his wife would sell me away from the people I loved.

This was when I learned more about the "underground railroad." It was a secret network of houses, carriages, and boats to help slaves escape.

My brothers and I tried to escape together, but after a while my brothers felt bad about the people we left behind so we turned back.

During the fall season of 1849, I didn't give up and eventually escaped again.

I followed the North Star all the way to Pennsylvania, traveling at night and staying at safe houses in the day.

When I found I had crossed that line, I looked at my hands to see if I was the same person.
NORTH

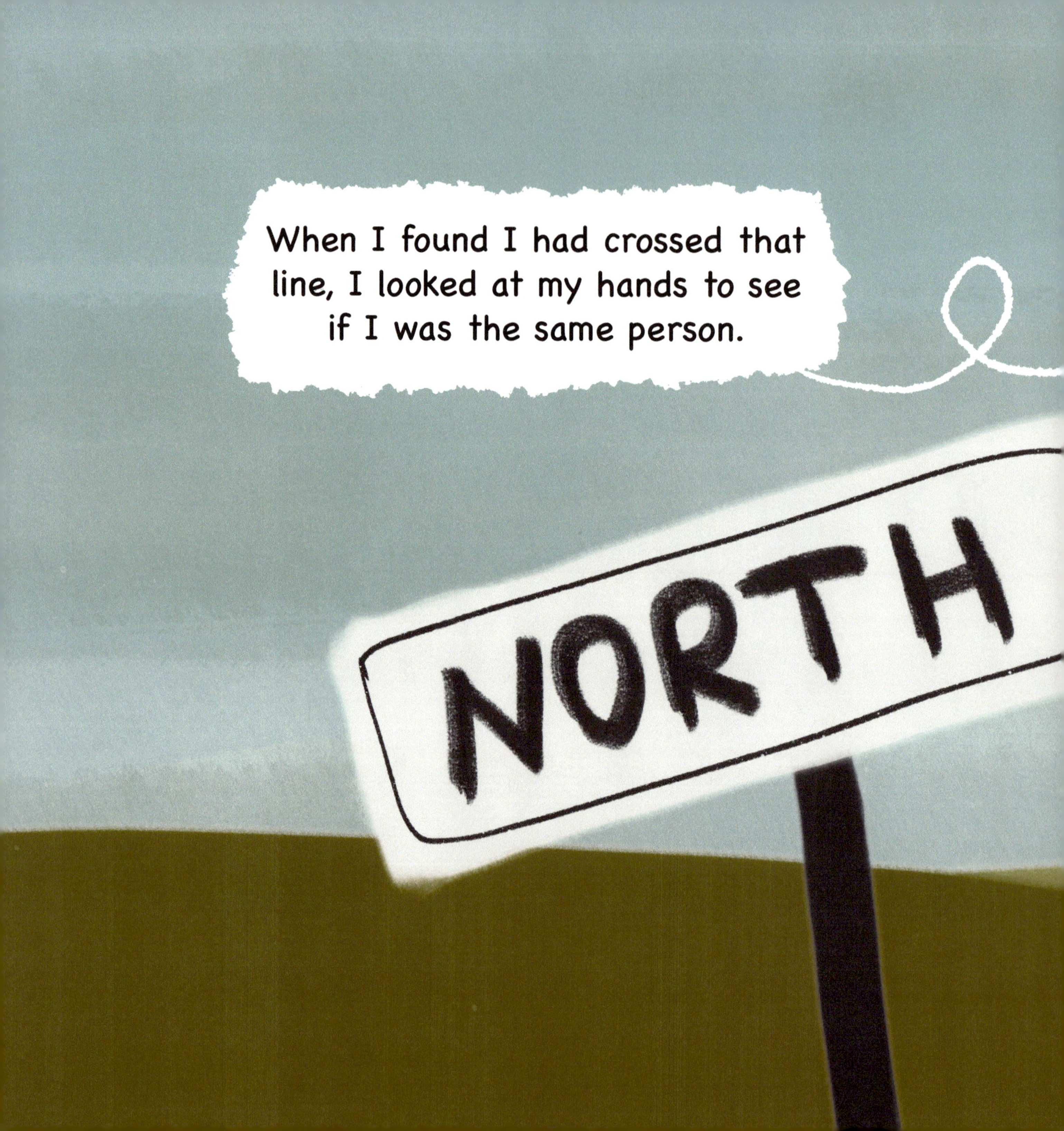

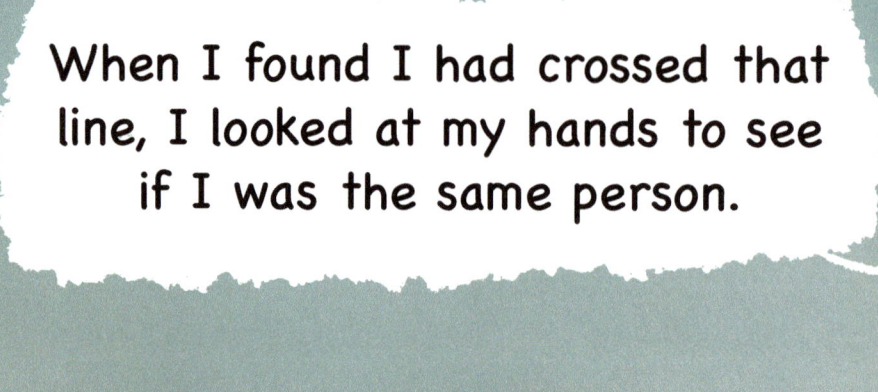

Afterwards, I traveled back to the south 13 times to help my family and other slaves escape.

Many people thanked and praised me, because I had given them hope and done what was thought of as unachievable.

I would give every drop of blood in my veins to free them.

In 1863, I led a group of scouts in confederate territory, and I nursed wounded soldiers in Virginia during the Civil War.

I liberated nearly 700 enslaved people during my time.

Once slavery was abolished, black men were able to vote, but women were not.

So, I joined a group to help women's suffrage by speaking out for women's right to vote. I shared the story of my life during and after the Civil War and stories of other women's suffrage to prove we deserved equality just as men.

In 1897, I was the speaker at the first meeting for the National Federation of Afro-American Women.

Timeline

1822 - Harriet is born into slavery

1844 - Harriet marries John Tubman

1849 - Harriet escapes to Pennsylvania for her freedom

1863 - Harriet becomes a scout, spy, and nurse during the Civil War, liberating 700 enslaved people

1897 - Harriet is the first speaker for the National Federation of Afro-American Women

minimovers.tv

 @marynhin   @officialninjalifehacks
#minimoversandshakers

 Ninja Life Hacks

 Mary Nhin   Ninja Life Hacks

 @officialninjalifehacks

www.ingramcontent.com/pod-product-compliance
Lightning Source LLC
Chambersburg PA
CBHW041521070526
44585CB00002B/38